THE
OTHER
SIDE
OF
OURSELVES

THE
OTHER
SIDE
OF
OURSELVES

Poems by

ROB TAYLOR

Cormorant Books

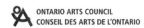

The publisher gratefully acknowledges the support of the Canada Council for the Arts and the
Ontario Arts Council for its publishing program. We acknowledge the financial support of
the Government of Canada through the Canada Book Fund (CBF) for our publishing activities,
and the Government of Ontario through the Ontario Media Development Corporation, an agency
of the Ontario Ministry of Culture, and the Ontario Book Publishing Tax Credit Program.

We gratefully acknowledge permission to quote "Untitled" by Al Purdy,
Beyond Remembering: The Collected Poems of Al Purdy, edited by Al Purdy and Sam Solecki,
Harbour Publishing, 2000. The ten lines appear as epigraph to the poem, "Lyric."

LIBRARY AND ARCHIVES CANADA CATALOGUING IN PUBLICATION

Taylor, Rob, 1983—
The other side of ourselves : poems / Rob Taylor.

ISBN 978-1-77086-009-4

1. Title.

PS8639.A9555075 2011   C811'.6   C2011-900014-8

Cover art and design: Angel Guerra/Archetype
Interior text design: Tannice Goddard, Soul Oasis Networking
Printer: Sunville Printco Inc.

Printed and bound in Canada.

CORMORANT BOOKS INC.
215 SPADINA AVENUE, STUDIO 230, TORONTO, ONTARIO, CANADA M5T 2C7
www.cormorantbooks.com

Contents

The Wailing Machines · 1

You Can't Lead a Horse · 2

The Horse Grazes · 4

The Diver · 5

Summer · 6

Old Men at the Community Pool · 7

Phantom Horses · 8

Early Rain · 9

Happiness · 10

The Party · 11

Morning After · 12

Shark Chaser · 13

Teaching Myself to Shave · 14

A Colouring Book · 15

A Diamond is For a Limited Time Only · 16

Squatter · 17

Nothing Against Art · 18

Death in Arcata · 20

The Way He Smiled Then · 21

The Night · 22

On Realizing Everyone Has Written Some Bad Poems · 24

Rejection Slips · 25

Haiku 1–4 · 26

Viaticum · 27

The Successful People of this World · 28

Spring Lament · 29

Errant · 30

Wintering   31

Creation Stories   32

Cross-Pollination   33

What the Minister Meant When He Said Love is Like a Flower   34

Tonight the Moon a Pie Tin Rinsed with Rain   35

Detritus   36

Wait   37

What Makes It Through   38

Advent   39

December Sonnet   40

The Great Ceiling   41

That One Semester   42

Upon My First Reincarnation   43

The Same Thing   44

Folding My Wife's Laundry   45

Computer Monitor Ekphrasis   46

To Be Familiar Enough to Name is Halfway to Death   47

The Slave Castle of Elmina   48

I Have Gone to Keta: Daytrip   50

In-Flight Movie   52

You Live For Me Here   53

Lyric   55

The Time of Useful Truths   59

Notes   61

Acknowledgements   63

The Wailing Machines

I wanted to say: look, this intersection, this place
where we have come together and stopped traffic,
is the only place we ever could have met, you and I —
pistons that never before aligned, even when the engine
was at rest, that had to wait until the whole contraption
burst and we were spilled out onto the pavement to see that yes,
all those hints — those darting noises, glints of steam and light —
held truth, that there are others as startled and ragged as ourselves,
and somehow gaining that knowledge seems worth all this blood
and bother and traffic lined up over the crest of the hill.
I wanted to say all of this, but my throat sputtered
which is why I merely waved as we were lifted away
and placed inside the wailing machines
we were only beginning to know to imagine.

You Can't Lead a Horse

On a blanket beside a river, lovers
listen to the silence of water.

All Gods, even the false ones,
are born from water.

Light will dance with many partners,
but none like water.

A newborn's heartbeat
is the sound of swirling water.

God's first decision:
to name the magma *water*.

In the lake's mirror, mountains wriggle
like jellyfish diving deep in water.

The priest needs the silver basin.
His God needs only the water.

A plane crash-lands safely on the Hudson.
No one thanks the water.

A blue whale's lungs are so large
they collapse without the support of water.

The woman is drunk.
She asks the water for waiter.

Trapped in sandstone for 10,000 years, raindrops
sometimes forget they are water.

When Patrick Henry said *liberty*,
he meant *water*.

The man ties his ankle weights
hastily. 'Not now,' says the water.

In five billion years the earth will be fire,
Europa will be a blue sphere of water.

What we speak is rocks.
What we cannot speak is water.

The sound of the boy's death moved through town
like a ripple of water.

The Horse Grazes

The horse grazes
in circles until there
is no more rope —

there is plenty
of rope, it is tied
to many things —

it is holding the
wind to the sky, the
horizon to the earth.

The Diver

He nears the crest of the waterfall,
friends circling in the pool below.
He is seventeen and almost comfortable,
caught in the middle of his last lazy summer.

He inches to the edge on stilt legs,
hunches his power-forward shoulders, peers
down. His friends hurl names at him
and he either listens intently or not at all.
In the moment it is hard to be certain.

He stands motionless for minutes.
His friends swim away,
leaving the deepest silence —
the kind that comes only with steady noise.

One day his father will die and he will suddenly be old,
a trap door released. Perhaps he is thinking of this.
Perhaps he is looking down at the pane of water
and imagining what his body will do to it.

I don't know or ask or gasp as he falls.

Summer

All day the phone rings. *Yes.*
Thank you. Not today. Please.
The kettle quivers. Tonight's chicken
puddles in its melt. Upstairs,
goldfish *o* the water's surface.
A forecaster's voice twirls
on the radio: *Sun, sun, sun!*
Outside, children buzz and loop
like model airplanes. Newspapers
crackle on the porch. A squirrel
scrambles up a bird feeder.
If someone doesn't pick
those zucchinis soon, they'll burst.

Old Men at the Community Pool

Smooth shapes here
and rutting thoughts —
the great interests of man.

Air and light curving
around young bodies, around
the joy of having a body.

They watch and grin,
the voluptuousness of looking —
their chest hairs drunk on jacuzzi bubbles,
their wives nearby, arms arcing
through miles of thirsty laps.

They rear up, motion
"five minutes" with open palms,
then dip back into this joy of air,
this voluptuousness of light.

Phantom Horses

The Poles at Krojanty taught us to get off the horses
and into something mechanical, riveted.
But what to do with the leftover horses?

Most of them are on traffic duty in European capitals,
a few in North America. Two of them patrol
the beaches of Vancouver after fireworks shows.

In the smoke and haze you hear first
the snorts from their powder clogged noses,
then there they are — looming shadows —

battalions of disoriented fireworks fans
scattering at the sight of these phantom horses
whose cinder-eyes flare, then drift out
as they wheel like tanks into the night.

Early Rain

At some point tonight this early rain
will swell and slip its ribbons
underneath our tent — it will pool,
pull the polyurethane fly
against the nylon shell
which will fall upon our bodies
and make of us one
slithering skin we'll shed
in the morning, split
then stuff into the hollow
wells of backpacks — the splash,
squelch of each footfall
from camp to lunch, a gray lick
under bloated oatmeal clouds
where we will argue over our mess
and the things we carry through it,
and will be no drier. But for now,
we lie silently beneath the beautiful
rhythm the sky is tapping
on the other side of ourselves.

Happiness

Happiness rushes in like a cat
you've forgotten outside in the rain.
Maybe you suddenly remembered him
or you happened upon him on your way
out to run an errand. Regardless,
your sin is forgivable as he is small
and stubborn and self-reliant —
you can't lose your life sitting silently
with him curled on your lap —
you would both quickly tire of that.
He shakes himself dry over the middle
of your rug, as though it were an innocent act,
and doesn't look at you. You walk alone
across the room, sit by the fire,
and wait there for the longest time.

The Party

I sought this guy out at the party
to thank him for the joke he'd told
at last year's party, which had served
as my icebreaker at every party since.
He vaguely recalled the party, me,
but the joke not at all. I recited the joke
and watched his confusion tumble
into a bottomless well of joy —
an Alzheimer's patient discovering
his own hidden Easter egg. *Good party*,
I said. *Good party*, he said.
Good party, I said to the hostess,
my hands excavating the mound
of coats on her bed. I hurried home
almost satisfied, rain lashing down on me
as it does after parties. I jangled my key
into the lock and the neighbour's dog
sprang up — *I'm here! I'm here!*
I'm here! I'm here! I'm here!

Morning After

Up of the down of the morning I spluttered
The jam of the table, the hardwood I buttered
The flop easy over, the quivering eye
The belly burst buzz of a swat-addled fly
The steam of the pot and the cot and the tongue
The slip of the pill and the swell of the gun
The shudder of water, the squeal of the truck
The hardwood I buttered, the marvellous fuck

Shark Chaser

For my father, shark repellent was power. He flew
bombing runs over the Pacific, confident in the lie
that if he crashed, the canister would protect him.

For our foreman, power was salmon: endless aisles of tins
stocked beneath the surface. When that promise
went to sea the last time, the lights in the cannery
flickered. Gathered on the floor, we expected each word,
yet could not contain our astonishment
as they splashed from his brackish mouth.

For us, power was paycheques. We stood dazed
in the parking lot, pink slips floundering in our palms.
Our wives wouldn't expect us for hours.
One of the guys decided to change
his oil and we circled around,
a gesture akin to friendship.

He tipped the can up, but nothing came.
He shook it and banged at it frantically,
then tossed it aside and laughed
three sharp bursts
which cut at the air like propeller blades —
the laugh you make but once in your life.

Teaching Myself to Shave

I was some generic hair growing age
and my Mom had already bought
me a pack of deodorants (when I'd
started to stink) which happened
to contain a little shaving kit.

So when my first stubble crept out of my follicles
I prodded at it with my fingers for a few days then
walked to the bathroom, lathered up the cream
and dragged the razor about,

then I threw on the aftershave
and didn't even scream
(though I was prepared to)
and wherever I cut myself
I put a dab of toilet paper,
just like Homer Simpson.

And that was that —
my stubble was gone,
my father was still dead
and the Sunday evening cartoons
weren't about to watch themselves.

A Colouring Book

My office is next to a kids' day camp
and from nine till three the noise is astounding,
but from three-thirty on, after the glue and glitter
have been scrubbed away and the last kid
(Timothy, it is always Timothy)
has been picked up, the whole building
is mine — which, like most things, is thrilling
for about seven minutes — after which I grow restless
and wander through the deserted rooms
where today I found a colouring book
opened to a picture of a wild-eyed man in a trench coat
and the statement "Because some people are evil,
you must never talk to strangers."

Someone had scribbled purple pencil crayon
over the wild-eyed man's face.

The frightening part was how I took the book
and tore it into pieces, my own eyes frenzied,
then buried it in a garbage can and walked
back to my office where I stayed until seven o'clock.

When I left there was only one other car in the parking lot:
a mother and her fourteen-year-old son sat inside.
He was crying so I didn't make eye contact.
Instead I drove until I was just out of their sight,
parked the car, and wrote this.

A Diamond is For a Limited Time Only

We would chip through granite
if we believed it buried beneath.
But what we desire is no diamond
stashed within the earth, no hidden
egg of light for us to hunt.
To dig it up and set it in a band
is to mistake one thing for another
as what we want cannot be fixed to anything
unless, like a fine-faceted thought,
it's fixed to every last thing there is —
a hopeless feat. Still, we have picks
and penknives and time to pass
and wherever there's a surface
there is something underneath.

Squatter

"Why here?" I screamed, my spit
speckling his face, my arms thrusting
east and west towards vacant plots.

 "There is a river," he said, "It wanders
slowly through your acreage. I listen from amongst
the poplars as it runs its fingers over the earth
and sings its inventory: *Here a stone, here
a bend, a bank.* When deer creep down
from the hills to drink, the river descants
tongue, tongue. At times, I strip off my clothes
and step in; the river searches for sheet music,
guesses I am a hoof, then when I pause to dive,
a rock. Finally, it realizes I am a fish, and falls
silent. It loves me then like a man loves a coin,
a brief possibility in his palm."

With this I slugged him to the earth. He spat
blood and dripped small, helpless tears.
Flecks of earth beneath him bloated black and set.
"I wish there was no river," he sobbed,
my boot rising to catch his lips.

Nothing Against Art

Nothing against Art Garfunkel
but I'd sucker punch the guy
if I ever got the chance,
really rattle his skull
and send what's left of his
ridiculous, frizzy hair
skittering into the air.

And even though some say
he is nothing more than
a tick engorged with
Paul Simon's blood,
he wouldn't deserve
the beating —

I mean, all he did
was move his lips
a little after Paul's
and in so doing create
the greatest harmony
the new world's heard
which hardly makes
him a parasite,
instead the lesser half
of a symbiotic relationship,
few of which are entirely
equal (long-beaked egrets
plucking bugs off the backs
of hippopotami, remoras
clinging to the underbellies
of indifferent sharks).

But this is hardly better, symbiosis
being a crutch of the beasts,
the animals that cannot
sustain themselves
inside themselves,
and Art Garfunkel's
career is the echo of
someone else's song,
a reminder of something
primitive and vital
that we muffle deep inside,
a voice which repeats
our joys and sorrows
one octave higher,
and asks us to listen —

a thing which I cannot
mute with my fists
so instead I dream
of punching Art Garfunkel
square in the face
and watching him fall
helplessly
to the ground.

Death in Arcata

Death comes slowly
to Arcata Plaza, but it comes
to All Under Heaven,
The Sidelines, The Alibi.

It's not a man in a cloak
or a suicide vest.
It doesn't bloom
like a mushroom
or squat outside TJ's
jangling coins in a hat.

It doesn't move toward you,
wash over you, touch you.
It only feels that way.

The last Saturday in September,
seven PM, leaving Mazotti's,
McKinley's shadow bending low
at his bronze hips, the sun a flame
over Rookery Books —

you suddenly desire
to lie in the cool emerald
snap of the grass,
and are not surprised by this.

> — *Arcata, California*

The Way He Smiled Then

Most chalked it up to delusion, deprivation,
the way he smiled then —
though at mass the next morning the priest
declared that it was the presence of the spirit
raising him for a moment before the fall,
and that night over beers Richard claimed credit,
arguing the guy'd recalled a dirty joke
Rich told on duty the night before.

But me, I think he was simply enjoying
the way the sun, dappled by clouds,
brushed against his skin, how the breeze
brought the freshest scents from the market
tumbling in over the stone walls,
how everyone had become temporarily quiet
and well behaved, his friends looking up at him
with a stoic moistness on their cheeks,
how it all came together so nicely
that even I, standing next to him,
rubbing the lacquered lever in my palm,
felt my face break out in a similar,
irresistible, grin.

Though no one remembers
that detail now.
No one asks me why.

The Night

When they came creeping
with knives gripped in their teeth
we were asleep, as they had planned.

Only three of us,
bunked furthest from the door,
were startled awake
by the startling of the others.
Only I escaped that room
with memories outlasting their blind cries.

How, I could not tell you if I wished.
But I remember, minutes and a mile later,
bending to wash blood from my hands
under the monochrome glow of the moon.
I remember how the darkness of the blood
relinquished the darkness of my hands
and snaked into the darkness of the lake.

I rubbed my face, my fingerpads
still puffed with sleep.
Had I survived, or been caught with the rest?
Was I still back there, dreaming —
a knife suspended inches from my throat,
a whispered signal stretching out across the room?

What woods had I just run through?
Whose blood had I seen slinking from my hands?

I told myself perhaps the other side
is like the night — darkness moving over darkness,
the things we think of as discrete
disappearing into one another.
I told myself perhaps the moon
is that unblinking light which lets us see
the layers of our living.
Or forces us.

I was too chilled, too adrenaline-
shot, too terrified to sleep.
And in this way I slept.

On Realizing Everyone Has Written Some Bad Poems

Another poem starts poorly, ends with pangs
of shame which cause my hands to reach out
like Purdy's hands snatching up loose copies of *The Enchanted
Echo* to later burn, or not (a good legend's never clear).

I read my poem and it bitters on my tongue
like the baking powder my father packed in pancakes
he poured and served out to us (unknowingly?) half-
cooked each early Sunday morning till his death.

I think of Purdy in his A-frame, midwinter,
low on firewood, a row of *Echo*es fading on the shelf.
Maybe he reached out his hands and grabbed them.
Maybe he let them be. I don't care which.

The choice matters, to be sure, splits hero from fool,
but it matters far less than its making.

Rejection Slips

Three this week, denying me cash
and a plumped CV to flash at perceived
opponents. My new hook, *Love*, as lureless
as the rest — and now, unemployed
and alone in our basement suite,
it seems this blind alley, this mess
of mixed metaphors, is the only theme I've left,
though today I try a turn at quiet desperation.

From bed this morning I heard you
over the shower's percussion, singing —
your voice didn't waver and for a moment
you were no woman I knew, or knew how to love,
and that awakening drew from me a tenderness
I can't describe. Which explains the rejections,
I suppose: I can never say what I intend.
This was to be a sonnet, for instance, and a lament.

Haiku 1–4

1

I can't help but hate
haiku. They end abruptly
just as they're getting

2

going. See? I need
another just to finish
this simple thought, and

3

maybe it's true that
all the love in the world could
fit in a matchbox

4

but who would want to
try, and where, in that case, would
one store their matches?

Viaticum

Do not worry. Everything you have wanted
to say has been said already,
the best of your thoughts cemented.
Do not worry, everything you have wanted
has been indexed and recounted.
Where you lie, relax, be steady,
do not worry. Everything you have wanted
to say has been said already.

The Successful People of this World

The successful people of this world
are always busy. They work all day
then come home and need to do something
so they cook the dinner, wash the car, cut the grass.

It's because of the successful people
that we have water restrictions:
this side of the street on even days,
that side on odd.

They like that kind of thing: a schedule,
they are usually big fans of schedules,
and when they have free time in theirs
they spend it composing new schedules.

When they take medication
they always put it in one of those plastic things
that divides the pills up by days.
In conclusion:

the successful people of this world
are busy and efficient, their actions
are their own rewards, and a green lawn
during a heat wave is their poem.

Spring Lament

By six the midnight frost has seen
the light and softened to its touch.
The black batons of wiper blades
have softened, too —
long gone the winter winds
that howled down and pinned
the wipers' stiffened backs
against the glass.
Now they slack, disperse
the crowd with casual
swings, even sing a little
as they go about their daily thrashing.

Errant

On the Internet tonight
I learn that in California
ten million tilapia
swim the Salton Sea. I turn
to tell you this, forgetting
you are gone. Outside,
a seven-thirty-seven rakes
the early evening air. A radio
spills its metal notes
into the yard; the neighbours
howl along, off key. Our landlord
slugs together mounds
of leaves and slime. It is October
and despite this the world
seems alive. The sun, recumbent,
lights a bowl of burly
apples in our red and orange
kitchen. The refrigerator hums
its love song to baking soda. My teeth
squeeze my lower lip. You are gone.
In real life, you will return
in seventeen minutes.
Here, I am not so certain.

Wintering

The key we'd hidden under a rock in the garden.
Our television,
laptop,
blender,
toaster oven.
One lamp,
two phones,
four shoes (not paired).
Half our CD collection (A–M, alphabetized).
The wood carving of a man in a canary yellow suit.
My watch and
my wife's jewellery:
the eleven necklaces her grandmother mailed her from Poland,
one each Christmas since she turned 13;
the bracelet I presented to her in high school,
so hideous she wore it only when she knew I was expecting it,
and even then only twice;
the dull ring she sported before I proposed
so the regulars in bars wouldn't slow as they passed our table.

And yes, all the abstract nouns you're expecting —
that flock of migratory starlings with quivering breasts.
They're gone too.

Creation Stories

She has her narratives, he has his,
and together they move through the world.

Their scripts are filled with the same set pieces, same characters,
yet they are blocked differently, recite different lines.

His parties end at 11:00, hers at 2:30.
They attend neighbouring churches, cheer for rival hockey teams.
She waters the lawn on Tuesdays, he mows it on Saturdays.
Their cars point in opposite directions each morning.
Their children attend different universities.

But we're only having one child, a girl,
he notes to her, drowsily.

She stares at the ceiling, smiles faintly.
It has taken so little for him to unmoor her.

Then our child will live on an island between us,
she concedes, rolling on her side.

And us? We will live an ocean apart?
He curls his arm around her, cocooning her in blankets.

He is long asleep before she can answer him,
but she whispers nonetheless, to the vaulted darkness,
We will beach ourselves upon her shore.

Cross-Pollination

The Pope would never approve
of how I pull these six desperate burrs
off my socks and drop them in the trash.
The least I could do, I know,
is toss them on the lawn
and give them a fighting chance
but then they might dig in and sprout
and I'd have even more of the
little bastards ravishing my ankles
every time I stepped out of the house.

I suppose I should be flattered
by my essential, polyester-blended role
in these plants' very survival
but from the way I clumsily hiked
behind her through the forest today
it seems abundantly clear
that I only have enough love
and energy to devote to one mate
and even that isn't enough sometimes
though I grasp onto her nonetheless
and hope that when she finally pulls me off
she places me down gently, in the earth.

What the Minister Meant When He Said Love is Like a Flower

Planted in darkness, it pokes up into your life
as a curious sound, a ticking which steadily
consumes. You search for its source and unearth
a bulb, its tight casing packed with wires
coiled around an explosive green heart
and timed by an internal clock you envision
as flame-red digits flaring, falling off.
You assess, attend to the unfurling mess,
spend what feels like decades studying
the bursts of leafing bundles which blur
into one mass you have to squint to separate
and ultimately, breathlessly, snip.
What follows, though, is worth the sweat and worry.
A moment's pause. A bloom.

Tonight the Moon a Pie Tin Rinsed with Rain

Safe beneath the broadest branch, I shook
the trunk then pecked the grass for bitter
little worm-battered apples destined
for sugar, butter, cinnamon, fire. I tossed them
in a painter's bucket, pausing only once
to raise a sample, plump and near-pristine,
up to the dull sting of early autumn sun.

I held it there a moment, turned it on my fingertips —
a simple gesture to fortitude and good fortune.
I could not yet understand, as I piled that apple
with the rest, that my gesture was one of many,
then, between sun, cloud, apple, hand, and eye —
was another of my overlooked lessons on love.

Detritus

Hand washing my favourite sheet pan for years,
new stains blend with old: caked sepia
creeping from the corners to a center
of swirled charcoal, and speckled atop, burnt
offerings to the god of good intentions.

Soaking does little so I cook on history,
which makes everything taste like dirt.

Sometimes I snap and pummel a metal mitt
of wool into the pan's pockmarked mug until my fist
bleeds a bit and the bakeware squeals for mercy,
spitting off isolate flecks of foodstuff —
a putrid little ticker-tape parade.

All the next week my meals sing the sting
of steel against my tongue, then I'm back at the sink
with my old problem and new scars.

Wait

Just before the anaesthetic set in, she whispered *wait*,
so he did.

His neighbours brought him fresh clothes and blankets.

Whenever one of the ward's patients was removed
the nurses offered him the unclaimed dinner tray.

On the third day they let him bring a couch in from the waiting room,
though this changed little.

To pass the time he spoke to her, softly describing
the comings and goings of the nurses,
the facets of the room
(the grey-diamond wallpaper,
the clock with the jammed second hand,
the flattened bottle cap he'd attempted to repair it with).

He tried once to finish a crossword puzzle, but gave up in frustration.

He came to the conclusion that he hated the English language
for all its ambiguous words.

He asked for a language of clarity, where *still* referred only
to the continuation of things and *wait*
meant she'd be coming back soon.

What Makes It Through

The baseball records don't
(often barely survive a season)
and with them fall peace treaties,
executive directives,
the plasterboard walls of libraries —
their horsehair insulation
spilling out.

They are followed by family
recipes, photographs, love notes,
that *oh* shape that bursts
onto your lips, sometimes.

Oh, the monumental lists we have written,
and will write again.

The other list, though, is simple enough:
a crystal decanter, a cracked mirror,
two necklaces, a broach,
a handful of rusty coins,
and that look the nurse gave
as she handed you the box,
perhaps.

Advent

On the bus home I watch the city, move away from it —
Starbucks, Tim Horton's, McDonald's, Starbucks.
I remind myself the world needs unbeautiful things —
it does not need poets, cannot sustain them. *And we don't want it to.*
I remind and remind;
snow considers falling.

Large packages jostle shoppers in and out of the neighbouring seats.
The hostages are polite today, apologise softly.
We need garbage men. We need physicists.

The blare of Chinatown gives way to East End Christmas lights,
patches of darkness. No one boards anymore.
We speed up, the city abandons its pursuit.

I stretch out my legs. *We do not need poets.*
Dangle my feet. *We need shoes.*

I am smiling as I step to the pavement.
Wind swirls behind the bus, dies away.
I smile at the woman with the sinuous walk. She smiles back, as always.
I smile at the boy on his way home from hockey practice, loaded with gear.
He is training for prehistory. His stick growls along the pavement behind him.
He watches me in silence, as if no longer afraid.

December Sonnet

What do a black guy and an apple have in common?
he slurs, steadying himself with his free hand
as the bus skids over the first thought of frost
which sprawls across the street and up the jittering
window I crack to drown the stink of spilled rotgut —
a sting of ice and pine ascends my nose and with it comes
the sudden memory of my father heaving a fresh-felled
spruce, cheeks flushed, into the truck bed — our two bodies
bouncing over logging roads, winter pressing its thin leaves
into the windshield — beaming in through the door
to my mother's approval and ornaments laid out:
packing-peanut garland, clothespin reindeer, egg carton bells,
and two bright baubles labelled HOPE and PEACE —
They both hang from a tree, he howls.

The Great Ceiling

Bowing to my wife's
bullying I bought
the doubly-expensive
spruce and shoulder-
slung it six blocks home
then dusted off
the cobwebbed stand
and squatted under
her surveyor's gaze,
twisting the screws —
I rose aching
to knuckle the knots
in my back but *quick*
she shot me a box
of bulbs and knick-
knacks which I unpacked
and hung one by one
before lifting
the cereal-top-tinfoil
star I'd crinkled together
our first Christmas
and tip-toeing it into place
just below the ceiling
and the great ceiling above that
where on the fourth day,
they say, the Man Upstairs
reached up and with
stretched fingers fixed
the constellations in their place,
then turned and, finding
no one to stand with
in that glow, slumped down
and started his new work
upon the earth.

That One Semester

I thought about the 95 Theses
and how scared Martin Luther must have been
with his wooden mallet and the weight
of an empire pinned to his vestments.

I thought about Plessy v. Ferguson
and being separately equal and equally separate
and how Langston Hughes taught me
that a black man can clean the pews of a white church
so long as he don't pray.

I thought about Robert Oppenheimer
and how he cried himself to sleep that night
when the sky glowed purple and soldiers
in bunkers two miles from the blast site
reported being able to see their own bones.

I thought about this whole God thing
and how maybe we've missed the point.
He isn't omnipotent or benevolent,
compassionate or clairvoyant,
he's simply there, all the time,
with a hammer and a broom
and frail human bones
flexing just under the skin.

Upon My First Reincarnation

Since coming back
I can no longer pick out death
from sleep, or wakeful sleep,
beyond a sense that two are short
and one is much too long.

Each waking brings a body, new,
oblivious of its abandoned others
except within its early morning aching:
the muscles' genealogy, a narrative
which does not care if it is heard
but tells and tells and tells.

I stretch my body, knead its sorest spots,
embroider it with clothes, compose myself, go out.

The Same Thing

My wife rises two hours before me each morning,
smacks snooze twice before I shove her out and sprawl
into her lingering warmth. She dresses in darkness, whispers
the bedroom door into the latch, pours milk over cereal and stares
longingly at the distant point in her mind where Clarity lounges
in its velvet slippers. Outside, she drops into our Cavalier and shifts
into gear. With this weapon she could kill, could turn south
and stick with it. Instead, she parks and punches in, prods numbers,
fidgets in an ergonomic chair, then heads home with the hope
that I've written a little something or at least have done the dishes,
which I haven't. I am not trying to say she is better than me.
I only mean to praise and wonder how love exists in muscles,
shadows, statistics, the screaming bellies of machines, and poems,
and is the same thing.

Folding My Wife's Laundry

Three weeks from now we'll ready for another summer wedding.
She'll lift her sundress from the drawer to find these spindly creases I cursed
but could not beat
splayed throughout its cotton folds and sigh the sigh that measures off
the distance between what is best and what today is good enough.

She'll guess I was distracted, which I was, though this time
taken by the lightness of her partner-in-grace clasped in my hands,
my clumsy thumbs
and fingers suddenly aware of the alliance they negotiate, the fragile limits
of curves. Each fold a compromise. Each smoothing sweep a prayer.

Computer Monitor Ekphrasis

Lean close enough to spot
the pixeled imperfections, hitches
for which there is no fix.

The scene we snapped, a trick
of bits and molecules
switched and stitched anew.

Click from shot to shot
from every stop along our lives
or pause and zoom on one.

Either way, in time,
the edges fray, the needlework
shows through.

That art's, like love, collaged
is hardly news. That what we say
and what we do are distances
apart, a simple fact.

The variations multiply,
but the archetypes stay few.
Lips, hands, hearts and eyes.
Red and green and blue.

To Be Familiar Enough to Name is Halfway to Death

I've walked foreign streets
studying every stone,
every vine that crept
through cracks, over walls.
I've stepped into rooms
I could never have imagined.

Now I live in a place
I call *home*,
a place I hardly remember
though I study
its television.

It tells me tonight how
parents can learn the sex
of their unborn child
earlier in pregnancy
than ever before.

Most are now named
before they are born,
half of the options eliminated
before their parents can see
their faces and realize
this is no *Timothy*,
this is no *Samantha*,
this is something entirely new,
something truly alive.

The Slave Castle of Elmina

We were led into the Condemned Men's Cell
and as the guide moved to seal the door
a woman in the group screamed and ran
out into the light of the courtyard shouting
that she'd felt something in there flying
back and forth between the stone walls
and sure enough when we quieted down
we could hear its faint cries and sense
its frantic little bird heart rattling in its cage of bones

so we all stood still in the musty darkness
as the guide described the last days
of rebellious slaves — how the soldiers
would put five or six of them in and not open
the door again until they were all dead
and I thought for a moment of that last man
waiting there with the bodies of his friends
(or, more terribly, strangers) arranged
in a row beside him — waiting —

but soon the guide reopened the door
and we stepped out carefully,
checking the soles of our shoes
for feathers, except one man
who waited motionlessly
until he could hear the bird well enough
to find it and cup it in his hands,
carry it out into the courtyard and send it
scrambling into the sky

and the next night over Chinese food
a friend asked me what I thought of
The Slave Castle of Elmina
and I shudder now because

all I could describe (before returning
to egg noodles and the clinking
of silverware on porcelain plates)
was the bird, the man's soft hands,
the woman screaming out into the sun.

— Elmina, Central Region, Ghana

I Have Gone to Keta: Daytrip

To Kobena Eyi Acquah, in response to his poem
"I Want to Go to Keta."

They are walking on water in Keta Lagoon
as we pull into town then cross the peninsula
to face the Atlantic from atop the boulders
they stacked here to fix the shoreline in this place
where we stand and watch the ocean swell in, then away
revealing chunks of concrete, shattered fingers
of rebar — startling in their permanence —

then turn and wander past what remains
of the half-drowned castle and children splashing
fine sand before it, chasing
a ball of vulcanized white gold
with sparks in their eyes

then on through the town
pocked with puddles and troughs
of water that expand with every turn
until the buildings give way to lagoon
sloshing among crumbling cement walls
and briny car parts and a man wading in water
up to his ankles who pulls small, netted fish
out of what was once his neighbour's living room
and smiles mildly, then turns away —
in the distance more men dragging
nets home, water shimmering
under their feet (a trick of the eye,
a flash of the miraculous that surfaces
in the mind at times then disappears below)

then back to the center of town
where the power remains off and lunch
is warm beer and biscuits at the pub
where drunks slam sticky handfuls
of banku onto our table and a miserably
sober man apologizes for all the drunks
and power outages and sloppy banku of Africa
then out again to the glare of the street,
towards the station, past the troop of glistening
boys back from the shore, shouting
and grinning, their ball skipping
ahead, a polished stone

and we are away, trotro engine thumping
and wheezing desperately as we plod
our course back to the mainland along
the edge of the now empty lagoon
the fishermen home with their children
and wives, who, I imagine, are rinsing
dishes and humming the tunes
to childhood songs whose words
they can no longer recall, whose melodies
they thought they'd long ago forgotten.

— *Keta, Volta Region, Ghana*

In-Flight Movie

The machinery of lift arrived too late —
millennia after the first sharpened tools,
first lives of fist, stone and gravity
dipped under the soil.
It took us far too long — our faith
calcified, weathered away —
and now, inside these metal angels,
we distract ourselves, fail
to scan the clouds for the beloved
we blessed and released into the earth,
the only place we knew to send them.

You Live For Me Here

You live for me
here

in the room of
my mind

one down from memory;
a room distinguished

from the others
by the bolted door

that guards it.
Sometimes I press

my ear against it
though I rarely hear

anything: a muffled
cough, the rustling

of papers. I know
this door so well —

it is larger than the
others, and warmer.

I fantasize that
behind it lies my

furnace (the secret
of its stoking

yours to maintain).
This is all I have of you:

the door, its heat,
the faith that

if I knocked,
you might answer.

Lyric

I am waiting for time to come
holding the many days' sameness inside me
fold on fold of invisible stuff
that you can't see and yet piles up
secretly in the mind like nothing at all
an unseen dust
*   — then I ask myself what I'm talking about*
and can't answer that either:
a quantity of something I can't describe
or measure or prove or disprove
                    — "Untitled," Al Purdy

On your day, my wife and I toss out
the words of a prayer for you, fourteen
years dead, a man she never met.
It's a blessing you said often.
Afterwards, I describe again
your broad chest and grin.
How you would have cared for her:
with *Warmth*, I say, with *Love* — words
I hope to one day enter, speak from.
I am waiting for time to come

and help me inhabit these words
you understood and lived:
Strength. Grace. Your last son
born late in life, something inside you
that could no longer be contained,
escaped as me. Your arthritic joints
supple as you supported my body
at swimming lessons, cradled its exhausted
looseness to bed each night. You firmly
held the many days' sameness inside me

and relished the repetitions:
What's this? Ball. *Good.*
Mama. *Good.* Papa. *Good.*
Words as wards against three waves
of chemo, the last the worst. Delusion —
your staccato stumbling from the mouth,
the earth. The losing rough as gravel,
steady as tides and tireless. Your mind and then
your body, one death not enough —
fold on fold of invisible stuff.

The importance I felt at your funeral
in my polished black shoes, the later
shame. The desert of middle school. First
crush, first shave, first awkward shiftings.
Always less remaining to forget:
a prayer, card game, story, your belly-flop
laugh. Then, high school's abandon. The girl
who will become my wife. Your slow burial
under new memories, muck
that you can't see and yet piles up

until the earth levels under short-trimmed grass.
Rituals each birthday, my arm slung
atop mom's shoulder. Later, my back hooked
over your version of solitaire, the game you failed
to beat in eighty years — a battle I resumed,
though I was satisfied with failure, a legend to recall
for my own children of the game no man could conquer,
not even their grandpa of mountains and myth
and genius. One story that wouldn't fail me, wouldn't fall
secretly from the mind like nothing at all.

That evening eight years in, eager
for sleep, I slid the pack out one-handed,
as you'd shown, and fanned the cards
across the table. Again and again the failure
of suits and numbers to find their common home.
I shuffled lazily, re-dealt, my thin hands heavy,
mind corroded by drowsiness and resignation.
Each move made with little calculation, care. Yet there
it was, the last card. Final thrust.
An unseen dust

rising off the pack. I searched
for my mistake. But no break in the pattern.
Everything in place but me, though I arrived,
thought of you sitting at the same table
years before. Your devout fingers.
Ruffled brows. Commentaries, in turns stout
and languorous. Apologetic chuckles.
Swift movements. Sweepings up. I spoke
these things aloud. In that room, I hauled them out,
then I asked myself what I was talking about.

The words hung dispossessed,
abandoned. Pride or shame or sadness —
anything but this absence, this wall
without a door. I pushed the cards away,
two-handed, then spoke the word *Death*
and watched it waver, a worn tapestry.
I asked myself how it meant, and what,
and why it had emerged from my body before *Love*.
I asked if it meant both or neither
and couldn't answer that either.

Your father was a good man,
says my wife, slipping her arm
across the small of my back and resting
it on the lip of fat above my hip. *Good.*
Yes, that's right. Of all the doors
I'd approached, but could not enter,
this one opens for me first. And across the room
another word, another door. And more.
Winding almost endlessly inside —
a quantity I can't describe.

Father, somewhere down this stretch of doors
is *Death*. Not at the end, but near it. *Love*
is further in, I fear. And *Fear*, yes, even further.
But how to navigate this path? A leaping, I suppose,
a stumbling. My thin hand in hers. A lifetime spent
opening one door, finding another. Each room tidy
and warm, prepared for our coming.
In thanks, we cast these words ahead across
the distance. If they reach, and whom, we cannot choose
or measure or prove or disprove.

The Time of Useful Truths

Ten years ago you fell for me because I told the truth.
Today truths trip me up at every turn, the only one
that matters long ago laid out and analyzed —
the tenor of its words, how *love* and *very*
vibrate in the caverns of our mouths and lungs
and ricochet through the resonant depths.

And yet here we're obsessed with tinny questions:
Do these jeans fit? Was that steak overcooked?
When the vacation, first house, first child?
What sex? What name? What if? And if? And later still?
And would you? How could you? Lie.

We lie. Beside each other, on the bed,
another shouting match flared out and set aside,
we sense the time of useful truths has passed us by,
left us but this one that comes in our shared silence —
at first it is the subtlest sound, then grows —
a decade's echo filling us with answers.

Notes

The italicized lines in "Old Men at the Community Pool" are by Mario Rossi, pulled from the epigraph of Wallace Stevens' "Evening Without Angels" as found in *Wallace Stevens: Poems selected by John Burnside*, Faber and Faber, 2008.

The title of "On Realizing Everyone Has Written Some Bad Poems" is a play on Al Purdy's "On Realizing He Has Written Some Bad Poems". The poem is dedicated to Al and Eurithe Purdy, and to the Al Purdy A-frame Trust, which is working to preserve Al and Eurithe's A-frame in Ameliasburgh, Ontario. For more information on the campaign, visit: http://www.harbourpublishing.com/PurdyAframe/

"That One Semester" is dedicated to Karen Ferguson.

"Computer Monitor Ekphrasis" was written as part of an ekphrastic writing collaboration between Pandora's Collective and The Sidney and Gertrude Zack Gallery. Thank you to both for the opportunity.

Keta is a town on the Eastern coast of Ghana. Located on a narrow isthmus between the Atlantic Ocean and Keta Lagoon, it is slowly being eroded from both sides. Kobena Eyi Acquah's poem "I Want to Go to Keta," referenced in "I Have Gone to Keta: Daytrip," inspired both my visit to Keta and the poem that resulted from that visit. Acquah's poem is from *The Man Who Died: Poems 1974–1979*, Asempa Publishers, 1984.

The Al Purdy epigraph for "Lyric" is from *Beyond Remembering: The Collected Poems of Al Purdy*, Harbour Publishing, 2000. Reprinted with permission. "Lyric" is dedicated to my parents.

Acknowledgements

I gratefully acknowledge the assistance of the BC Arts Council.

Earlier versions of poems in this book have been published in the journals and magazines *ACTA Victoriana*, *The Antigonish Review*, *Contemporary Verse 2*, *Eclectica*, *The Feathertale Review*, *High Altitude Poetry*, *OCW Magazine*, *Prairie Fire*, *Quills*, *Red Fez*, *Riddle Fence*, and *subTerrain*, and in the anthology *Rocksalt: An Anthology of Contemporary BC Poetry (ed. Mona Fertig and Harold Rhenisch)*.

"Lyric" was first published as a chapbook in Fall 2010 by *The Alfred Gustav Press*. Thank you to press founder and editor David Zieroth for giving me that opportunity.

"You Can't Lead a Horse" was co-winner of *OCW Magazine*'s 2010 Poetry Contest, and an earlier version of this book, under the title *The Wailing Machines*, won the Writers' Federation of New Brunswick's 2010 Alfred G. Bailey Prize for best unpublished manuscript. Thank you to these organizations and their judges — the encouragement you gave me was greatly appreciated, and put to good use.

Many, many people helped in the composition of *The Other Side of Ourselves*, and I have no hope of thanking all of them. A particular thanks, though, to Paddy Chitty, Steven Heighton, Aislinn Hunter, Sandra Lloyd and Karen Solie. And a big thank you to Robyn Sarah, who was the kind of unsparing and considerate editor I always hoped I'd one day have the chance to work with.

Thank you to my friends and family, my father and my mother. And of course, of course (did you think I'd forget?), to Marta, for making my life so complete that I can do frivolous things like breathe and eat and write poems.

About the Author

Rob Taylor was born in Port Moody, British Columbia, and now resides in Vancouver with his wife, Marta. He has travelled widely, most recently to Ghana where he co-founded *One Ghana, One Voice*, Ghana's first online poetry magazine. His poems have appeared in over forty journals and anthologies, including *Prairie Fire*, *Riddle Fence*, *The Antigonish Review*, and *Rocksalt: An Anthology of Contemporary BC Poetry*. An earlier version of *The Other Side of Ourselves* won the 2010 Alfred G. Bailey Prize for best unpublished poetry manuscript.

Author photo by Marta Taylor.